ANIMALS IN THE WILD

ASIAN ELEPHANT

Annette Whipple

A Crabtree Forest Book

Crabtree Publishing
crabtreebooks.com

Notes for Readers and Class Discussion

This book is designed to teach readers about core subject areas, build curiosity, and inspire further investigation. Readers are encouraged to build upon what they already know about the subject and engage in topics they want to learn more about. Here are a few guiding questions to prompt reflection and discussion. Possible answers appear in red.

Before Reading:

Read the title and look at the table of contents. What do you already know about Asian elephants?

- *I know that Asian elephants are smaller than African elephants.*
- *I know that Asian elephants live in groups called herds.*

What would you like to learn about Asian elephants?

- *I would like to learn about how much food an Asian elephant eats in a day.*
- *I would like to learn whether the Asian elephant is endangered.*

During Reading:

Pause after reading each page or chapter. What questions do you have about what you read? What are you curious to know?

- *I wonder why adult Asian elephants have no natural predators.*
- *I am curious to know what other animals are considered megaherbivores.*

Make connections to what you are reading. How is this like something you already know?

- *I know that some animals, including hippos and rhinos, use mud to protect their bodies from the Sun.*
- *I know that many animals communicate with each other using smells.*

After Reading:

Recall key details about the book. What was the author trying to teach readers?

- *The author was trying to teach readers about the characteristics, behaviors, and habitats of Asian elephants.*
- *The author was trying to teach readers that Asian elephants are an endangered species and at risk of becoming extinct if they are not protected.*

How did the images and captions help you understand more?

- *The photographs helped to show me how Asian elephants interact with each other in the wild.*
- *The captions helped me understand new details about Asian elephants.*

Table of Contents

Meet the Asian Elephant

What's the largest living land animal in Asia? The Asian elephant! This massive mammal lumbers through tall grass at the edges of forests and stands taller than humans.

Elephants are the largest terrestrial, or land, animals.

Adult Asian elephants average 11 feet (3.5 m) in height. African elephants are more than 13 feet (4 m).

Look-a-Likes

At first glance, Asian elephants look like their African elephant cousins, but they are different. Asian elephants don't grow as tall and have noticeably smaller ears. Only a small number of Asian elephants grow **tusks**, but nearly all African elephants do. Even their trunks and heads are different in shape. Unfortunately, all elephants are **endangered**.

Mammals

Asian elephants are mammals. All mammals share some of the same characteristics. They keep a constant body temperature even as their environment gets warmer or colder. Hair or fur covers their skin. Females give birth to live young and feed their young with the milk the mother produces.

Chapter 1

What Do They Look Like?

Asian elephants grow to an enormous size. On average, adults weigh between 7,500 and 11,500 pounds (3,400 and 5,200 kg).

Elephants take mud baths to distribute mud—or "nature's sunscreen" on their sensitive skin. They also use their long trunks to lift and place mud on their bodies—like humans use their hands to rub on sunscreen.

Big and Strong

Asian elephants' unique bodies support their massive weight. Their **dense** bones handle great amounts of pressure because of their size. Long bones and strong muscles provide leg strength. Thick pads cover the bottoms of their feet and absorb stress and shock while they walk.

Tough-Skinned

Asian elephants are known for their thick, tough skin. The skin on their backs measures about 1 inch (2.5 cm) in thickness. Numerous **nerve endings** make an elephant's skin very sensitive. Asian elephants use dirt, sand, and mud to protect their skin from insects and the Sun.

The ears of Asian elephants are smaller and more rounded than African elephants' ears. This is an **adaptation** because they live in cooler climates than their African relatives.

In a Flap

To cool itself, an Asian elephant flaps its ears. Blood rushes through the blood vessels in the ears. The blood cools down. Then the cooled blood moves through the elephant's entire body and cools the elephant by several degrees. This is called thermoregulation.

In the Trunk

The elephant's long nose and upper lip combine to form its trunk. The trunk has no bones, but it's loaded with muscles and nerves. An Asian elephant's trunk lifts heavy objects with ease. It uses its trunk to eat, communicate, sort, spray, and lift. The end of its trunk has a single "finger." It helps the elephant to understand the world and to explore with precision.

An elephant's trunk is prehensile, meaning it is able to grasp or hold.

Tusks

Tusks are special kinds of teeth that grow from some elephants' upper jaws. The long tusks are hard and white like bone, but made of **ivory** instead. Most Asian elephants never develop tusks, but some males have large tusks that never stop growing. They grow about 7 inches (18 cm) each year.

Tusks protect the trunk, move objects, dig holes, and gather food. Elephants also fight using their tusks.

Elephas

Asian elephants are the only living members of the *Elephas* genus, or group, of animals. They are more closely related to mammoths than to African elephants. Mammoths were huge, hairy elephantlike animals that died out about 4,000 years ago. *Elephas* originated in sub-Saharan Africa millions of years ago. Modern Asian elephants **evolved** from a species of *Elephas* that **migrated** to the Indian subcontinent.

Chapter 2

Home and Habitat

Asian elephants are native to South and Southeast Asia. They range from India in the west to Indonesia in the east.

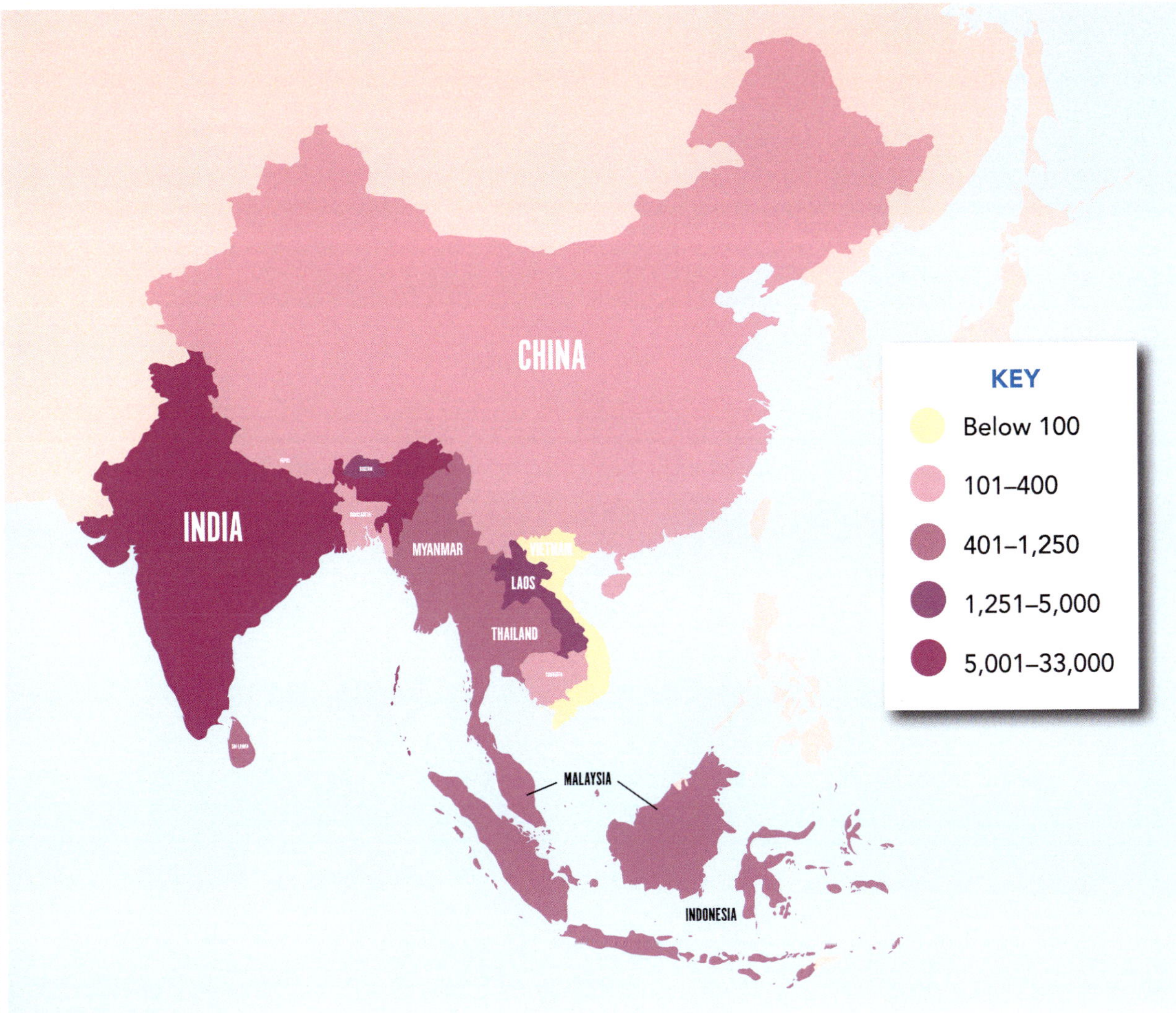

Subspecies

There are three **subspecies** of Asian elephants. They are the Sri Lankan elephant, the Indian elephant, and the Sumatran elephant. These Asian elephants live in about a dozen countries throughout the large continent of Asia. More than half of wild Asian elephants currently make their homes in the country of India.

Shrinking Range

In the past, Asian elephants lived widely throughout much of Asia. They roamed the continent south of the Himalayas and into China. Their distribution is much more limited now, in isolated pockets of grassland and forest **habitats**.

Follow the Food

Asian elephants live in a variety of habitats, including tropical evergreen forests, dry and wet deciduous forests, grasslands, and scrublands. They also range along the borders of cultivated, or farmed, lands. They migrate from one area to another as needed, searching for their favored vegetation, or plant life, and water. After **foraging** for a couple of days in one area, they move on. They typically travel between 1 and 4 miles (1.6 and 6 km) in a day.

Asian elephants are considered **megaherbivores.** They graze and browse on hundreds of pounds of plants each day.

In the Loop

Asian elephants tend to move through their home range in a loop or circuit. Home ranges can vary in size, from as small as 6 square miles (16 sq. km) to larger than 500 square miles (1,300 sq. km). Multiple herds of Asian elephants can overlap ranges. The range size depends on the amount and quality of food, as well as how many other male bulls and female cows are in the area.

Herds usually consist of cows and calves. Bulls roam alone, but sometimes come together. These are known as bachelor groups.

Humans and Elephants

Asian elephants have a long history of human interaction. Bones of ancient Asian elephants have been found at archaeological sites in the Indus River Valley. They were used as working animals and even in armies at war in ancient civilizations. Today Asian elephants are the national animals of Thailand and Laos. In India, they are national heritage animals. Despite their historic and cultural importance, their populations suffer today because of human interactions and conflicts, as well as human-caused habitat loss.

An estimated 3,783 Asian elephants live in **captivity** in Thailand—that's more than the wild population. Logging has destroyed much of their wild habitat. The captive elephants live in camps. Some are kept as tourist attractions.

Grazing in the Grass

These forest animals spend most of their days eating grass. They are easier to spot in open grassy areas. Dense forest habitats don't provide enough vegetation for Asian elephants to eat, so they leave the forests for grassy areas close to forest edges. Asian elephants escape to the forest shadows to avoid the hot Sun.

Chapter 3

What to Eat?

With their massive size, it's no surprise that Asian elephants spend about two-thirds of their days eating. They can eat more than 300 pounds (136 kg) of vegetation a day.

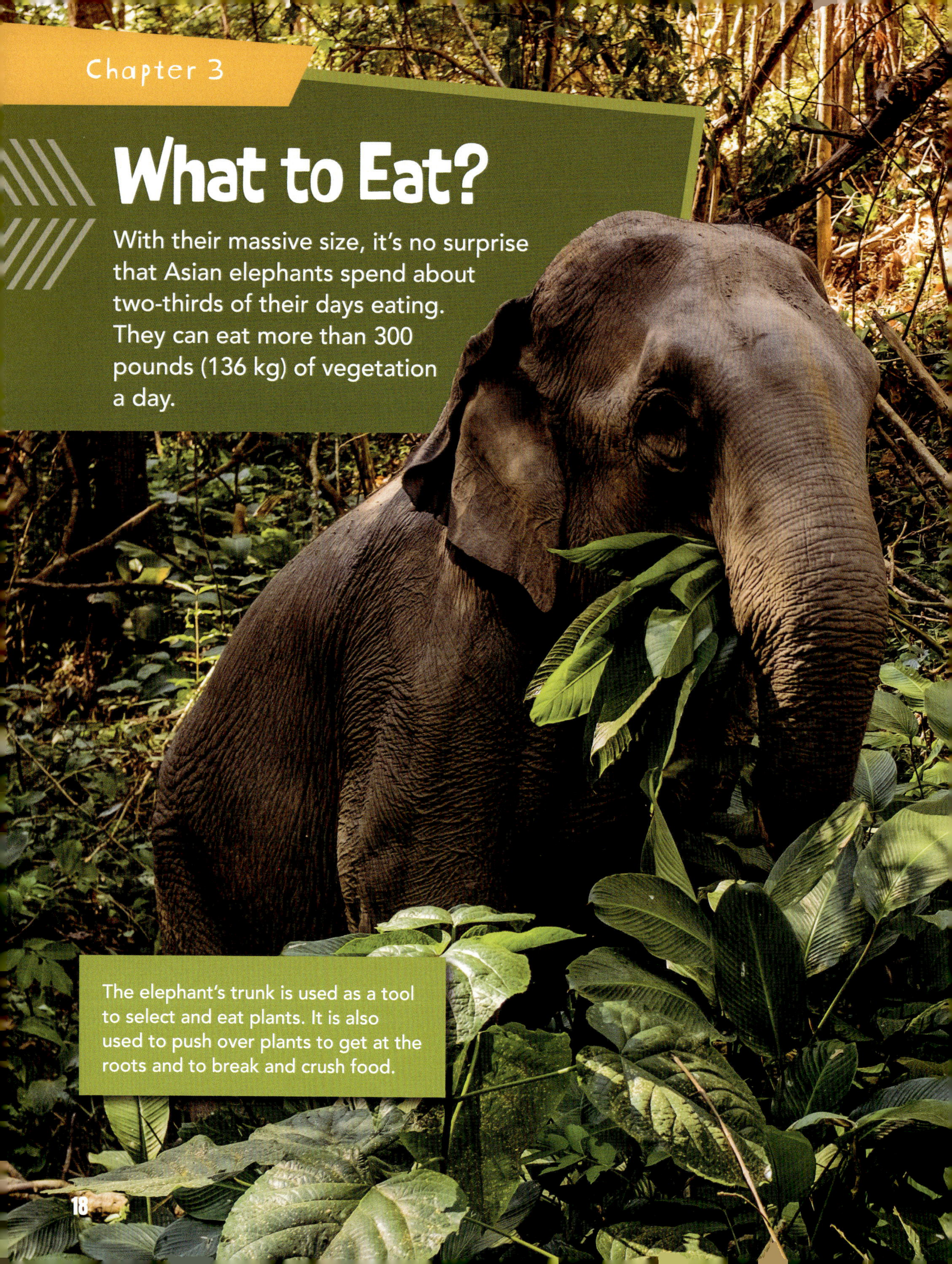

The elephant's trunk is used as a tool to select and eat plants. It is also used to push over plants to get at the roots and to break and crush food.

Asian elephants can make tools out of chewed bark to plug holes in the ground and keep water from evaporating.

Eat to Live

Asian elephants gather wild grasses as they walk. They pluck the grass from the ground with their trunk. The trunk passes the grass to the elephant's mouth to chew. They also eat leaves, roots, bark, and fruit.

Varied Diets

Wildlife biologists who study Asian elephants have noted they have "regional preferences" in the food they eat. This means they tend to eat specific foods in different geographic areas. In southern India, they eat more than 100 plant species, while in Borneo, they eat more than 180. In Nepal, they eat more than 60 plant species. In China, biologists have observed Asian elephants eating around 100 plant species. In Malaysia and Sri Lanka, Asian elephants eat 200 to 300 different plant species.

Elephants are great problem solvers—especially when it comes to food. They use their trunks to pull down high tree branches.

Dietary Needs

Studies show that Asian elephants have to eat large amounts of food because their **digestive systems** are not efficient. They can feed—taking small mouthfuls at a time—for 12 to 18 hours a day. They eat in the morning and evening when it is less hot.

Grab and Go

In addition to grasses, their trunks grab leaves and strip bark from trees. They also eat roots and stems of plants. Grains such as wheat and millet, root vegetables such as cassava and pumpkin, and fruits such as mango, jackfruit, and papaya, are also favorites.

Teak, palm, bamboo, and rubber trees are often damaged when elephants forage for their preferred foods.

Elephants need minerals such as salt and calcium. Mineral deposits are often found near water sources.

Water Babies

An elephant drinks up to 55 gallons (208 L) of water a day. That's more water than a bathtub contains. Water is necessary for their survival. The elephant's trunk holds about 2 gallons (8 L) of water. This huge animal squirts water into its mouth to drink—and to cool itself.

Shrinking Food Sources

Over time, humans have taken over more and more land that Asian elephants used to freely roam. The land is used for farms and homes. With less land available to them, these animals sometimes eat farmers' crops. This causes conflict with farmers, who often consider elephants pests.

Asian elephants change their eating habits according to the season. In the dry season, they browse plants. In the wet season, they eat grass during the early rains when it is more **nutritious**.

Chapter 4

Asian Elephant Behavior

Asian elephants are social animals. Most live in herds for their entire lives and they form strong family bonds. They are known for being affectionate, or loving, and for showing grief when a member of their herd dies.

Food is more available in Asian elephant habitats and there are fewer **predators** than in African elephant habitats. This means individual Asian elephants make more independent decisions.

Female Asian elephants recognize each other even after long separations.

Family Affair

Small social groups of Asian elephants work together as families. These family herds include about 15 female adults in a group plus their related offspring. Young, or immature, males are also part of the group. Adult females are **predominant** in the herds. But they don't have a true **matriarch** leader like their African cousins.

The Importance of Relationships

Relationships are important to elephants, and they play a key role in behavior. The adults in a herd raise and protect the young together. As highly social animals, all Asian elephants frequently touch one another with their trunks.

Multiple Communication Modes

Elephants are very intelligent animals. They communicate in ways that humans don't yet fully understand. They interact using body posture, or the positioning of their bodies. Some of these postures are so subtle that researchers often miss them while studying Asian elephants in the wild.

Elephant Calls

Asian elephants communicate with one another with sounds as well. They chirp when nervous. Their loud trumpet calls show excitement. They also growl, squeak, and snort. Over long distances, elephants use low-pitched sounds as alarm calls.

Even with years of study, biologists don't know everything about Asian elephant dominance hierarchies, or who leads a herd and why.

Young are disciplined with a touch. They compete and fight with one another by touching as well.

Asian elephants also communicate with touch. They greet one another, play, and show excitement through touch.

Playing to Learn

One way elephants transfer knowledge is through play. They play to learn. They use tools for work and even create their own tools. Research suggests elephants also demonstrate **compassion**, sorrow, and self-awareness. With poor eyesight, elephants rely on their other senses. Touch and hearing are important for their survival.

Predator Alert

When a member of the herd senses a predator, she sends out a low-pitched warning. These rumbles can be heard and understood by elephants more than 2 miles (3 km) away. The adults surround the calves, and they all run for safety while protecting the most vulnerable. When threatened, Asian elephants run with their tails held high.

Scent Communication

Chemical smells called **pheromones** provide scent communication. Smells in pee and poop leave messages. One elephant leaves a scent behind. Other elephants use their trunks to sniff fluids left on natural surfaces—or on the elephant. Then they know more about the elephant.

Elephants are crepuscular. This means they are more active at dawn and dusk, when it is cooler. They sleep about four hours each night—most of that while standing.

Pooping for the Environment

Asian elephants poop a lot! They poop every two hours and up to 15 times a day! About 50 percent of what they forage is digested. The lower-quality foods pass through their digestive systems quickly. This large amount of poop helps the environment in many ways. Some smaller animals such as deer, mongooses, and birds feed on the seeds in elephant poop. They in turn **disperse** the seeds in their own poop—helping to spread plants across a wider region.

Dung beetles use elephant dung, or poop, for food and nesting.

Chapter 5

The Next Generation

Wild Asian elephants are long-lived animals, living from 60 to 70 years. As adults, they breed every four to five years. They have one baby at a time—twins are rare—and usually nurse them for two to four years.

Mating Signals

Elephants use pheromones to communicate about **mating**. The female cow urinates, or pees. The urine includes chemical scents that tell other elephants she's ready to mate. The male bull smells her scent message with **olfactory receptors** in his trunk. Then he communicates through his own behavior. If he's ready to mate, he moves closer to the cow and her urine.

If he's not ready to mate, a bull might act shy or uninterested by moving away from the pheromone signal.

Mating Age

Cows are mature enough to produce offspring around 10 to 15 years of age. Bulls tend to mature even earlier. However, both usually wait several more years to mate. Males need to be strong enough to dominate other males before mating. When ready to mate, bulls have a burst of **testosterone**. They wander around looking for females and often become aggressive. They fight other males.

Musth for Life

Male Asian elephants go through a period where their reproductive hormones increase and they become restless and more aggressive, or likely to attack. This is called musth. Musth is a word that means **intoxication** in the Urdu language of South Asia. These bulls produce more testosterone at this time. Musth signals a bull's intent to mate. It also makes them restless and violent—sometimes to other elephants and humans.

Bulls in musth produce a thick, tarlike substance called temporin. It oozes from the temporal glands near their cheeks.

Age and Musth

Musth starts when a bull is around 20 to 30 years old and continues until they are about 50. Male elephants go through musth for up to three or four months a year. Bulls in musth make a low rumbling noise that other Asian elephants can hear from miles away. Cows that are ready to mate will reply back with their own sounds, while other elephants avoid these bulls.

Birth and Babies

Once a female matures, she can give birth every three to four years. Pregnancy lasts for 18 to 22 months before a calf is born. Asian elephants typically give birth to just a single calf—it is difficult to feed two and twins don't always survive in the wild. A newborn calf stands soon after its birth. It weighs a whopping 200 pounds (91 kg). Hair covers the body of the baby. This hair darkens and thins as the calf gets older.

Calves hold the tail of their mother for comfort, security, and affection.

A Family Affair

A calf nurses, or drinks milk, from its mother and even other females in the group. After several months, the calf begins eating grass. It continues to nurse for up to three years. Interestingly, a calf also eats its mother's dung. This provides the calf with nutrition, as well as helpful bacteria that aids digestion.

Born with Teeth

An Asian elephant calf is born with six sets of small teeth. As the elephant gets older, the teeth move forward. Most female Asian elephants and some males have tusklike teeth called tushes. Tushes are made of a brittle type of ivory. They are often used as tools to dig in the ground or strip bark from trees. Some male Asian elephants develop tusks from their upper jaws.

Only about 50 percent of Asian elephants develop tushes.

Long Lives and Memories

Asian elephants can live 60 years or longer in the wild. However, in captivity they face a lot of problems. Fewer calves are born. Sometimes calves are removed from mothers too soon. Sadly, there are times the elephants aren't cared for appropriately and are even mistreated. In captivity, it's a challenge to provide Asian elephants with the exercise they need.

Chapter 6

Asian Elephant Conservation

Adult Asian elephants have no natural predators. However, the young are attacked by tigers and lions. Humans and human actions are the Asian elephant's biggest threat. Wild elephants try to avoid people. But if they feel threatened, they are likely to charge.

Loss of Territory

Habitat loss due to human expansion into Asian elephant territory has led to the fragmentation, or breaking up, of their habitat. When elephants search for food in these fragmented territories, they often damage or eat agricultural crops. This leads to human–elephant conflict.

Asian elephants have lost much of their habitat to **deforestation**. People cut down forests for logging and firewood.

The trade in elephant ivory is banned or restricted in many countries. But the illegal **poaching** of elephants and trade of tusks and tusk powder continues.

Endangered Species

The trade in Asian elephant ivory was banned in 1975 but there is still an underground trade in elephant tusks. They are used in traditional medicines and for carvings and jewelry. Asian elephants are listed as endangered by the International Union for Conservation of Nature (IUCN) Red List. This is a list that assesses and ranks the **extinction** risk of animals and plants. The Red List is used by governments and organizations to develop laws and **conservation** practices that protect endangered animals.

Elephants can cause up to 3 million dollars in damage each year, making them an enemy to farmers and agriculture.

Ancient Connections

Elephants have a long history with people. These animals are part of many Asian cultural traditions. Many ancient Asian and South Asian myths, stories, art, and music feature elephants. In times of war, the use of elephants helped armies appear threatening. Elephants' massive size also made them useful as work animals for transporting, hunting, and pulling heavy loads. Elephant keepers called mahouts still train them in some countries where elephants have become tourist attractions.

Asian elephants have good memories for words and melodies. They can follow dozens of spoken commands, which helped make them useful as battle elephants.

Elephant Conservation

Some researchers think fewer than 52,000 Asian elephants live in the wild. Their population is further endangered by conflict with humans over grazing lands, and poaching. Land reserves have been set aside, but they're often too small to accommodate elephants' needs. **Natural corridors** allow animals to move to different habitats that would otherwise be isolated from one another. The Jakarta Declaration for Asian Elephant Conservation is an agreement to protect these elephants. It was signed in 2017 by 13 countries where the elephants range.

As people develop forests and open lands, Asian elephants lose their home ranges and migratory routes. They lose access to water and the vegetation they need to survive.

adaptation (ad-uhp-TEY-shuhn): A change in an animal or plant that makes it better able to live in its habitat

captivity (kap-TIV-i-tee): When an animal lives under human control or care

compassion (kuhm-PASH-uhn): A feeling of caring about the suffering of others

conservation (kon-ser-VEY-shuhn): The protection of animals, plants, and their habitats

deforestation (dee-fawr-uh-STEY-shuhn): The permanent clearing of forests or large areas of trees

dense (dens): Having parts that are tightly packed together with little space in between

digestive system (dahy-JES-tiv SIS-tuhm): The set of organs in the body, including the stomach and intestines, that turns food into energy and nutrients

disperse (dih-SPURS): To spread or scatter over a wide area

endangered (en-DEYN-jerd): An animal or plant species that is considered to be at a very high risk of becoming extinct in the wild

evolved (ih-VOLVD): Changed gradually over a long period of time to survive better in an environment

extinction (ik-STINGK-shuhn): When an animal or plant species completely dies out and disappears from Earth forever

forage (FAWR-ij): To search for food

habitat (HAB-i-tat): The place where an animal or plant naturally lives and grows

intoxication (in-tok-si-KEY-shuhn): When an individual's mind or body is affected by something they have consumed, or taken in

ivory (AHY-vuh-ree): A hard white material that forms the tusks of elephants and other animals

mate (meyt): When a male and female animal join together for the purpose of producing offspring

matriarch (MEY-tree-ahrk): A female who controls a family or group

megaherbivore (meg-uh-HUR-buh-vawr): A large plant-eating animal that weighs more than 2,200 pounds (1,000 kg)

migrate (MAHY-greyt): To move from one area to another at different times of the year

natural corridors (NACH-er-uhl KAWR-i-dawrs): Designated areas of land and water that allow animals to move safely between habitats

nerve endings (nurv EN-dings): Points all over the body which send messages to the brain about sensations such as heat, cold, and pain

nutritious (noo-TRISH-uhs): Containing substances that a person or animal needs to be healthy

olfactory receptors (ol-FAK-tuh-ree ri-SEP-ters): Cells in the body that receive smells

pheromone (FER-uh-mohn): A chemical substance that an animal produces to communicate with other animals of the same species

poach (pohch): To catch or kill an animal illegally

predator (PRED-uh-ter): An animal that hunts other animals for food

predominant (pri-DOM-uh-nuhnt): Being more important or noticeable

subspecies (SUHB-spee-sheez): A smaller group of animals or plants within a species

testosterone (tes-TOS-tuh-rohn): A chemical substance produced in the body that is responsible for many of the physical characteristics specific to adult males

tusk (tuhsk): A long pointed tooth that sticks out of the mouth of some animals, such as elephants and walruses

INDEX

COMPREHENSION QUESTIONS

1. True or False: All Asian elephants grow tusks.

2. Newborn Asian elephants typically weigh around ______.

   a. 50 pounds (23 kg)
   b. 100 pounds (45 kg)
   c. 200 pounds (91 kg)

3. True or False: The trunk of an Asian elephant has no bones.

4. To cool itself, an Asian elephant ________.

   a. flaps its ears
   b. puts mud on its skin
   c. eats lots of grass

5. True or False: Asian elephants are nocturnal, or most active at night.

6. Asian elephants are considered _______.

   a. megaherbivores
   b. ultra-omnivores
   c. ubercarnivores

7. True or False: Asian elephants are an endangered species.

8. Wild Asian elephants typically live for ________ years.

   a. 25–30
   b. 60–70
   c. 90–100

ANSWERS
1. False, 2. c, 3. True, 4. a
5. False, 6. a, 7. True, 8. b

About the Author

Annette Whipple is the author of many children's books, including *The Laura Ingalls Wilder Companion: A Chapter-by-Chapter Guide, Whooo Knew? The Truth About Owls, and Quirky Critter Devotions: 52 Wild Wonders for Kids.* When Annette's not reading or writing, you might find her baking for her family in Pennsylvania. Get to know her at AnnetteWhipple.com.

Written by: Annette Whipple

Editor: Ellen Rodger

Proofreader: Melissa Boyce

Design and layout: Tammy McGarr

Production manager: Candice Campbell

Image Credits

Shutterstock: KobchaiMa p 23 (background), Dan Campbell p 41 (top)

Wikimedia Commons: Creative Commons p 34, p 35, Public Domain p 42 (inset photos)

All other images from Shutterstock

Crabtree Publishing

crabtreebooks.com 800-387-7650

Hardcover 978-1-0398-7479-4
Paperback 978-1-0398-8433-5
Ebook (pdf) 978-1-0398-8192-1
Epub 978-1-0398-8312-3

Published in Canada
Crabtree Publishing
616 Welland Avenue
St. Catharines, Ontario
L2M 5V6

Published in the United States
Crabtree Publishing
347 Fifth Avenue
Suite 1402-145
New York, New York, 10016

Library and Archives Canada Cataloguing in Publication
Available at Library and Archives Canada

Library of Congress Cataloging-in-Publication Data
Available at the Library of Congress

Printed in the U.S.A./CP022026